YOU ARE ANSWER TO SOMEONE'S *Prayer*

YOUR EXPERIENCES QUALIFY YOU
TO ANSWER SOME OF
LIFE'S TOUGHEST QUESTIONS

Esther Maurice

AuthorHouse™
1663 Liberty Drive
Bloomington, IN 47403
www.authorhouse.com
Phone: 1 (800) 839-8640

Published by AuthorHouse 02/20/2019

ISBN: 978-1-7283-0072-6 (sc)

Library of Congress Control Number: 2019901847

Print information available on the last page.

Any people depicted in stock imagery provided by Getty Images are models, and such images are being used for illustrative purposes only. Certain stock imagery © Getty Images.

This book is printed on acid-free paper.

authorHOUSE®

Move, Do *something,*
A *small* step
or a *huge* leap,
regardless,
you *won't* be
in the same place
you were yesterday.
#PursueYourPurpose
#EMM

Esther Maurice

DEVOTIONAL:

TODAY, DO NOT ALLOW YOUR LAUNDRY LIST OF "THINGS TO DO" INTIMIDATE YOU. YOU HAVE A LOT TO ACCOMPLISH BUT EVERY LITTLE STEP COUNTS. BE INTENTIONAL TODAY AND MAKE IT A PRIORITY TO SET 15-30 MINUTES ASIDE TO WORK ON YOUR PASSION. WRITE IT DOWN, MAKE A FEW CALLS, NETWORK… DO SOMETHING. EVERY STEP BRINGS YOU CLOSER TO YOUR GOAL.

WHAT WILL YOU DO TODAY TO MOVE YOU TOWARD YOUR GOAL?

_____

_____

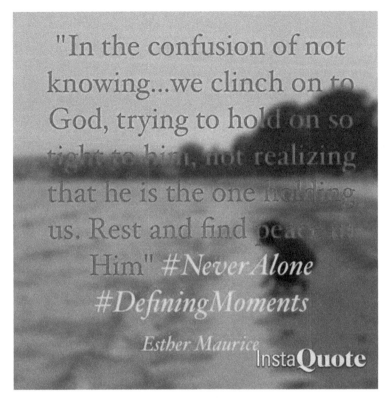

> "In the confusion of not knowing...we clinch on to God, trying to hold on so tight to him, not realizing that he is the one holding us. Rest and find peace in Him" *#NeverAlone #DefiningMoments*
>
> *Esther Maurice*
>
> InstaQuote

DEVOTIONAL:

FEAR, THE BIGGEST ENEMY TO YOUR PURPOSE AND TOO OFTEN THE MOST VICTORIOUS. GOING AFTER YOUR GOALS AND DREAMS TAKES COURAGE. OFTEN TIMES WE HIDE BEHIND OUR FAITH IN GOD, AS IF HE IS GOING TO BE THE ONE TO WRITE THE VISION AND WORK ON THE PROJECTS. YOU HAVE ALREADY BEEN EMPOWERED WHEN YOU WERE INSPIRED. IF HE CALLED YOU TO THE TASK, HE'S WITH YOU ON THE MISSION! GO, BE GREAT!!

1 TIMOTHY 3:17

WHICH ONE OF YOUR FEARS WILL YOU CONQUER TODAY?

_____

_____

WE OFTEN PRAY AND ASK GOD TO MOVE
ENEMIES AND ROAD BLOCKS OFF OF OUR
PATH, OFTEN TIMES NOT ADDRESSING
THE FACT THAT WE MAY BE PART OF THE
SETBACK, THROUGH OUR EGOS, OUR FEARS,
OUR DOUBTS OR JUST OUR BAD HABITS. MY
PRAYER TODAY IS "GOD MOVE ME OUT OF
MY WAY!"

ESTHER MAURICE

DEVOTIONAL

DO NOT ALLOW YOUR EGO, YOUR FEAR, YOUR DOUBT OR YOUR BAD HABITS
TO HINDER YOU FROM RECEIVING ALL THE GREAT THINGS GOD HAS IN STORE
FOR YOU. LEAVE SOME SPACE FOR UNDERSTANDING OTHERS, COMPROMISE AND
CHANGE. BE INTENTIONAL IN MOVING OUT OF YOUR OWN WAY.

LIST YOUR TOP THREE, EGO TRAITS, DOUBTS AND FEARS THAT USUALLY GET
IN YOUR WAY.

HOW WILL YOU BE INTENTIONAL TODAY TO MOVE OUT OF YOUR OWN WAY?

_____

_____

Hang Up the Gloves
Let Their Hate
Activate Your Love
LOVE ALWAYS WINS!!!

DEVOTIONAL

You will not always be celebrated. Often times the ones you thought would celebrate seem to be the biggest obstacle. They may "hate" but do not engage simply keep moving in love. Love always wins. The hate only comes to distract you from your goal. Keep moving, when they can't beat you, they usually join you!

AFFIRMATION:

Today, I will focus on My Goal. I will not be distracted by those who aren't cheering me on, Today I will encourage myself.

There's a blessing
in submission.
Honoring someone
that can lead, advise,
rebuke, love and
strengthen you.
It births humility.
It's not about knowing
all the answers,
but the one you submit to,
may have all the right questions.
#ThinkAboutIt #Submission

Esther Maurice

DEVOTIONAL:

Do you have someone in your life that can hold you accountable? Someone that can challenge you? There is a blessing in submitting to someone you can trust with your successes and failures. Being humble enough to submit and follow not only strengthens you, but it reveals your capacity to lead. You may have all the right answers but to the wrong questions!

Who do I trust enough to submit to? Why?

_____

_____

Change what YOU can't accept

Accept only what God Allows!
#fearless #KeepPushing

Esther Maurice

DEVOTIONAL

Separation, whether permanent or temporary, is often part of the process of moving into your new season. However, be mindful because everyone does not have to leave as an enemy. Accept the change in relationships. Hold on to the good, forgive the bad and celebrate new beginnings. Change what you can't Accept, accept only what God Allows. Pray for the wisdom to know the difference. #ItsForYourGood

AFFIRMATION

Today I will trust that any changes, good or bad, will still work out for my greater good!!

As you pursue your purpose and expect God to open doors, you must accept that He will close some doors as well.

#ItsForYourGood

Esther Maurice

<u>DEVOTIONAL</u>

Just as God is opening doors for you in some areas, you must expect and accept that He will close some doors as well. You are transitioning into a new season of your life and relationships built during that transition period is vital. Knowing the difference of those meant to stay requires wisdom, faith and courage; wisdom to decide where the relationship will go, faith that making you're making the right decisions and courage to stay or walk away. Stay true to your character and keep moving forward. Those meant to go with you, will.

DEVOTIONAL

You may not always be able to answer "why" you are faced with different situations, but just remember there is lesson in it. You will not come out the way you went in. Be wiser. Be stronger. Be better! This is what qualifies you to be the answer to someone's prayer!

The test is not given to destroy you, it's here to develop you.

Esther Maurice

SELF-CHECK

What particular challenges are you facing today? How do you believe this will develop you?

_____

_____

DEVOTIONAL

Stop waiting for permission to move forward. The fact that you want to go forth means You already have the courage and strength to take the next step!

AFFIRMATION:

I do not need anyone's permission to be Great!

DEVOTIONAL:

TALK TO GOD AND COMMAND YOUR DAY!

*Dear Lord,
I invite you to be with
me on today.
When I feel like giving up
remind me how precious life is,
When frustration tries to creep in,
let peace overshadow
When something comes
to make me angry,
let me think of something
that makes me laugh uncontrollably.*

*When hate presents itself, Let love prevail..
And when this day ends let me rest knowing
I've lived, I've laughed and I've loved
and tomorrow is an opportunity to do it again .
Amen.*

AFFIRMATION:

TODAY I ENCOURAGED BECAUSE I KNOW SOMEONE IS PRAYING FOR THE GIFT GOD HAS PLACED IN ME. I AM THEIR ANSWER!

DEVOTIONAL:

THEY ARE ALWAYS WATCHING! BE MINDFUL OF YOUR WORDS AND ACTIONS.
MORE PEOPLE LOOK UP TO YOU THAN YOU KNOW!

SELF-CHECK

DESCRIBE YOUR PICTURE OF TODAY.

_____

_____

DEVOTIONAL:

The world is waiting to meet the REAL you! You are too awesome to deprive the world of meeting the gift of you. God considered all your flaws and imperfections and still decided to place someone's answer within you! Your Transparency will win their trust and reveal their prayer.

Psalm 139:14

SELF-CHECK

How will you re-introduce the real you to someone today?

_____

_____

DEVOTIONAL:

You've come farther than you think! Forward movement is movement, regardless of the distance. Celebrate small victories; they are the building blocks to the next platform.

Zecheriah 4:10

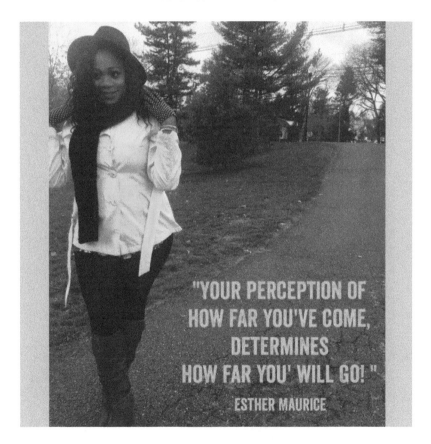

"YOUR PERCEPTION OF
HOW FAR YOU'VE COME,
DETERMINES
HOW FAR YOU' WILL GO!"
ESTHER MAURICE

AFFIRMATION:

Today, I celebrate my progress. I am one step closer to fulfilling my goals because I am not where I started.

DEVOTIONAL:

YOU DO NOT HAVE TO ANSWER EVERYTHING THEY SAY ABOUT YOU. THE ADVANTAGE YOU HAVE OVER GOSSIPERS, HATERS AND MANIPULATORS, IS THAT THEY ALWAYS UNDERESTIMATE HOW MUCH YOU REALLY KNOW. SO DON'T GET DISTRACTED, STAY FOCUSED. GIVE THEM THE GIFT OF YOUR SILENCE FOR NOW. YOU'LL KNOW EXACTLY WHEN TO SPEAK AND MORE IMPORTANTLY EXACTLY WHAT TO SAY WHEN THE TIME IS RIGHT! KEEP PUSHING!

JAMES 1:19

AFFIRMATION:

TODAY I WILL PRACTICE THE ART OF LISTENING!

DEVOTIONAL

I PRAY YOU FIND PEACE TODAY. IN THE MIDST OF ALL THE CHAOS AND NOISE OF LIFE, MAY YOU NEVER FORGET THAT GOD IS STILL GOD. YOU HAVE ACCESS TO SOMEONE THAT IS BIGGER THAN YOU. YOU DON'T HAVE TO CARRY THE WORLD NOR DO YOU HAVE TO HAVE ALL THE ANSWERS. AS YOU MOVE FORWARD, TRUST THAT JUST AS HE PROVIDES ALL THAT YOU NEED, HE HAS PROVIDED YOU HIS PEACE AS WELL. RECEIVE IT.

PSALM 46:10

WHAT SITUATION WILL YOU ALLOW HIM TO CONTROL ON TODAY?

_____

_____

DEVOTIONAL:

God is still working on you. You're not a finished product but everyday strive to do your best, to be the best you!!

Philippians 1:6

AFFIRMATION:

I am a child of God. I am not perfect, but I am unique, I am evolving and I am loved.

DEVOTIONAL

As you pray and trust God, be sure to pay attention to what He is doing or who He is sending into your life. Don't miss it. You're answered prayers may not look the way you expected.

AFFIRMATION:

Today I will be intentional in expecting that God will answer my prayers!

WIN!!
NEVER LOSE SIGHT OF YOUR GOAL!
KEEP PUSHING!
ESTHER MAURICE

DEVOTIONAL

DON'T GIVE UP! YOU HAVE COME TOO FAR TO GIVE UP NOW. THERE'S A PURPOSE TO YOUR PAIN. I PRAY YOUR STRENGTH TODAY TO CONTINUE TO FIGHT THE GOOD FIGHT OF FAITH. REMEMBER THAT THE FIGHT IS FIXED! YOU WIN!

SELF-CHECK

WHAT HAS BEEN YOUR BIGGEST OBSTACLE THUS FAR?

_____

_____

Sometimes you just have to Hold on to your Hat & Go for the Ride!

Esther Maurice

DEVOTIONAL:

WE ALL LIKE TO BE IN CONTROL, BUT THERE ARE CERTAIN SITUATIONS, WHERE YOU CANNOT TAKE THE LEAD. OFTEN TIMES YOU JUST HAVE TO GO THROUGH THE PROCESS. TRUST THAT GOD WILL LEAD YOU AS YOU BECOME A FEATHER IN HIS WIND. FIND GOD IN EVERY CIRCUMSTANCE. YOUR PAIN IS NOT WITHOUT PURPOSE.

DECLARATION:

MY PURPOSE, MY PAIN AND MY TRIALS WILL PRODUCE THE ANSWERS THAT SO MANY OTHERS SEEK!

DEVOTIONAL:

Everyday we wake up go to work, school or just handle basic life needs. Not often do we take the time out to rest, meditate or even hear the voice of God. At some point in the midst of all the chaos there has to be a moment where we can put down our phones and lay down the heavy burden that we carry daily. A time where you can just go before God, vulnerable, weak and tired and accept that it is okay. A time where you can go to be rejuvenated, refreshed and cast your all cares to Him. These days we all seem to wear a cape and have this superhuman strength to go on and on and on without ever taking time to be replenished. We all need a time to rest. A part of being strong is having the humility to say "I need a break" and "Lord I need you". So today I pray that you cast your cares unto Him and allow him to strengthen and comfort you. Knowing that your weariness or frustration, doesn't make you weak, it's a reminder that's you're human. Let Him renew your strength.

ISAIAH 40:29 ; ISAIAH 40:31 ; MATTHEW 11:28

DECLARATION:

I WILL NOT FEEL GUILTY WHEN I NEED TO REST.

THE DARKEST HOUR IS YOUR OPPORTUNITY TO SHINE THE BRIGHTEST!

ESTHER MAURICE

DEVOTIONAL:

Facing difficult times can cause us to lose hope & the will to keep pushing. But today I challenge you to change your perception and see your darkest hour as an opportunity. An opportunity to learn and start fresh, if necessary. An opportunity to be your best even in the worst of times. A star shines the brightest in the dark. So look around, and notice the other stars around you. You're not in this alone.

Matthew 5:16

DECLARATION:

Today I will be the star that brightens someone's day !

DEVOTIONAL:

LOVE IS AN ACTION WORD!

1 CORINTHIANS 13

SELF-CHECK

HOW WILL YOU EXPRESS GOD'S LOVE ON TODAY?

_____

_____

Sometimes we are so focused on the people God has allowed to leave us that we overlook those He has allowed to stay. #MoveForward

Esther Maurice

DEVOTIONAL:

Focus on the present and move forward! It will make sense soon enough. Enjoy & appreciate those that are still with you. Do not allow bitterness, anger or hurt to keep you stuck in the past. Whether their departure is temporary or permanent, God allowed it to happen. Dig deep and find the strength to continue to move forward. Don't miss out on the present because you're lost looking in the past.

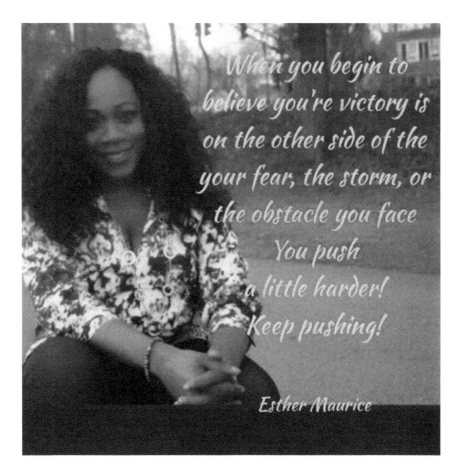

When you begin to believe you're victory is on the other side of the your fear, the storm, or the obstacle you face You push a little harder! Keep pushing!

Esther Maurice

DEVOTIONAL:

Keep pushing! These tough times are defining moments when you get to know you and God. Your weariness and weakness is just a reminder of how much we need God to strengthen us. These moments build character and You have come too far to give up now!

Joshua 1:9

DEVOTIONAL:

Don't give up, Create new lanes if necessary but don't you dare give up!

Philippians 4:13

DECLARATION:

I am not built to quit!
Make a list of your top three goals!

WE ARE ALL SUPER
IN SOME ASPECT TO THOSE AROUND US.
BUT FINDING THE ONE
THAT LOVES THE CAPE,
RESPECTS THE CAPE,
BUT REMINDS YOU
THAT YOU DON'T NEED IT,
IS PRICELESS!

DEVOTIONAL

WE ALL DESERVE TO HAVE THAT SOMEONE IN OUR LIVES, WHO KNOWS HOW STRONG WE ARE BUT ALSO PROVIDES A SAFE PLACE FOR OUR WEAKNESSES. ONE THAT DOESN'T REQUIRE YOU TO KNOW EVERYTHING, DO EVERYTHING OR SAY ALL THE RIGHT THINGS BUT LOVES THE YOUR SUPERNATURAL CAPACITY AND YOUR HUMAN LIMITATIONS.

REFLECTION:

WHO CAN YOU TRUST ENOUGH TO LEAN ON??

SO...
WHO ARE YOU??...
WHAT DO PEOPLE GET
WHEN YOU WALK INTO
A ROOM??
#PURPOSE
#SELF-LOVE

ESTHER MAURICE

DEVOTIONAL:

WHO ARE YOU?? MOST OF US DO NOT KNOW HOW TO ANSWER THIS QUESTION. WE TELL PEOPLE WHAT WE DO BUT NOT WHO WE ARE. YOUR CHALLENGE FOR TODAY, ANSWER THIS QUESTION!

SELF-CHECK

WHAT DO PEOPLE GET WHEN YOU WALK INTO A ROOM? (SUGGESTION: ASK SOMEONE CLOSE TO YOU.)

_____

_____

YOU are the ANSWER to Someone's PRAYER!

@thesthermaurice

DEVOTIONAL

Someone is counting on the purpose God has placed in your life. Don't think that your gift is so small that it won't be a blessing to others. You are an answer to Someone's Prayer!

DECLARATION:

I Am the Answer to Someone's Prayer !

EVEN WHEN YOUR AUDIENCE DOESN'T CLAP, KEEP MOVING, THEY ARE STILL WATCHING....

ESTHER MAURICE

DEVOTIONAL:

WHETHER THEY CLAP OR NOT, DO NOT LIVE YOUR LIFE BASED ON THE APPLAUSE OF OTHERS. YOU MUST REALIZE THEY ARE STILL WATCHING AND THE "SHOW" ISN'T OVER. SO KEEP MOVING, ENCOURAGE YOURSELF AND WATCH THE REAL SUPPORTERS STAND AS YOU WORK YOUR PLATFORM!

SELF-CHECK

HAVE YOU BEEN SECRETLY WAITING FOR A "THEIR" APPLAUSE TO MOVE FORWARD?

_____

_____

THE JOURNEY, NOT A DESTINATION, REVEALS ALL THE BEAUTIFUL SHADES OF YOU! #PROCESS #PURPOSE #SELFLOVE #EMM

DEVOTIONAL

DON'T DESPISE THE PROCESS, IT REVEALS THE STRENGTH, WISDOM, POWER AND BEAUTY YOU POSSESS TO OTHERS AND MORE IMPORTANTLY TO YOURSELF.

SELF-CHECK:

HAVE YOU BEEN SO BUSY COMPLAINING ABOUT THE PROCESS THAT YOU HAVEN'T LEARNED FROM IT?

_____

_____

WHY TAKE A STEP, WHEN YOU CAN LEAP!!

ESTHER MAURICE

DEVOTIONAL

Have enough Faith to take a Risk. If we were to calculate and measure every single step we would have no need for Faith. So trust God and trust the gift he placed in you!! You already have the answer!!

SELF-CHECK:

How will you LEAP today?

_____

_____

DEVOTIONAL:

As we work on our goals and take leaps of faith, one of our most common worries are financially driven. Worry of how we will fund this great vision God has given us. I challenge you today to continue to build the vision. Explore the resources around you. Everything you need to get through today was already prepared yesterday. Find it!

Enjoy Today. Live, love and laugh, everything will work out.

Matthew 6:24

Embrace the Peace
God has already
given you.

Esther Maurice

John 14:27

DEVOTIONAL:

PEACE: THE MOMENT WHEN NOT ONLY THE OUTER NOISE IS SILENCED BUT THE INNER TURMOIL HAS SUBSIDED. DON'T ALLOW THE CARES OF THIS WORLD TO OVERTAKE YOUR MIND. THERE WILL ALWAYS BE A PRESSING MATTER THAT COMES TO DISTRACT YOU FROM EMBRACING THE PEACE THAT GOD HAS ALREADY GIVEN YOU. SO TODAY, BE INTENTIONAL IN NOT BEING OVERWHELMED.

IT'S GOING TO BE OK.

Just because they know your Past doesn't mean they get to dictate your future!

Esther Maurice

<u>DEVOTIONAL</u>

Don't let those that knew you "when" dictate your "now". People often try to incarcerate us by our mistakes, short comings and so-called secrets they have about us. Guess what....They don't get to decide when you are free to move forward. The past is just that, the past. Learn from it, grow from it, forgive, love & move forward. Take into consider that they can not envision your future because they are the ones stuck in the past. So don't keep them company, just continue to pursue your purpose with passionate! You can show them better than you can tell them.

Your quality that Attracts People and the one that makes them stick around can be two different things.

Esther Maurice

DEVOTIONAL:

TWO OF THE MOST IMPORTANT THINGS YOU CAN LEARN ABOUT ALL YOUR RELATIONSHIPS ARE: WHAT ATTRACTED SOMEONE TO YOU AND WHY THEY ARE STILL AROUND? KNOWING WHAT OTHERS EXPECT FROM YOU WILL HELP YOU TO DEFINE HOW THEY SEE YOU. THIS GOES BEYOND THE SURFACE OF "I LOVE YOU" BUT CHALLENGES YOU TO FIND OUT WHAT KEEPS THEM DRAWN TO YOU. IS IT YOUR HUMOR, YOUR WAY OF THINKING, YOUR HONESTY; IS IT SEX, IS IT MONEY? WHAT IS THE FOUNDATION THAT UNDERGIRDS THE LOVE THEY HAVE FOR YOU? THEN ASK YOURSELF, IF THAT FOUNDATION IS MOVED, IS THIS LOVE STRONG ENOUGH TO STAND?? WHETHER WE ADMIT IT OR NOT WE ALL HAVE A SOMETHING WE LOVE & EXPECT FROM OTHERS. LOVE YOURSELF ENOUGH TO BE HONEST ABOUT THE MOTIVES OF YOUR RELATIONSHIPS. MANY RELATIONSHIPS ARE STRAINED BECAUSE THEY ARE EXPECTING SOMETHING YOU'RE NO LONGER WILLING TO GIVE. LOVE YOURSELF ENOUGH TO GET SOME ANSWERS.

DEVOTIONAL:

Often times we focus so much on the ones that are winning that we never consider its because they know what it feels like to lose... and guess what???.... they don't like the feeling! It's about understanding the necessary sacrifices and making them. Our daily challenges can be so overwhelming that we often lose our passion to pursue our vision & lose our desire to win. Don't be so defeated that you don't ever fight again. Just learn from your loss, get back up and go for what God purposed in your heart!

James 1:12

SELF-CHECK:

Have you allowed a recent loss, cause you to quit?

_____

_____

THAT VOICE
THAT TELLING YOU,
"YOU CAN'T MAKE IT",
IS LYING!!!
PUSH THROUGH IT!!

DEVOTIONAL

TUNE OUT THE NEGATIVITY. EVEN WHEN YOU DOUBT THE PROMISE OR YOUR STRENGTH TO ENDURE, YOU'VE COME TOO FAR TO QUIT. SO FOCUS AND PUSH THROUGH THE PAIN, THE HURT, DROWN OUT HECKLERS. IF YOU KEEP GOING EVENTUALLY THEY WILL BE BEHIND YOU!

PHILIPPIANS 4:13

SELF-CHECK

WHERE IN THIS JOURNEY, HAVE YOU ALLOWED DOUBT TO SPEAK LOUDER THAN YOUR FAITH?

_____

_____

DEVOTIONAL

TRUE LOVE WHEN PRESENT ALWAYS PREVAILS. IN ORDER FOR IT TO PREVAIL IT MUST BE TESTED, OPPOSED AND CHALLENGED. SO TODAY, LET LOVE BE YOUR GUIDE. ONE DAY YOU MAY BE IN NEED OF THE LOVE YOU'RE CHALLENGED TO GIVE, SO BE INTENTIONAL AND WALK IN LOVE, SPEAK WITH LOVE, AND BE THE MOST AUTHENTIC EXPRESSION OF LOVE.

SELF-CHECK:

IS YOUR CAPACITY TO SHOW LOVE BEING CHALLENGED?

_____

_____

Balance.

BE COMMITED WITHOUT BEING CONSUMED

WE OFTEN GIVE SO MUCH TO THE TASK, TO FAMILY, TO WORK OR MINISTRY THAT WE LOSE SIGHT OF WHO WE ARE IN THE PROCESS. FROM THE NEVER ENDING "TO DO" LISTS, TO THE IMPROMPTU DEMANDS, WE ARE BUSY WITH FINDING ANSWERS FOR OTHERS THAT WE LOSE WHO WE ARE IN THE PROCESS. THE CHIPPING AWAY IS SO GRADUAL AND THE FALL IS SO SLOW, THAT BY THE TIME YOU REALIZE HOW MUCH YOU HAVE LOST AND HOW FAR YOU HAVE FALLEN YOU'RE IN A PERPETUAL STATE OF "HOW DID I GET HERE?" SO TODAY I CHALLENGE YOU TO FIND YOU AGAIN. FIND YOUR JOY, DIG DEEP FOR THAT SMILE YOU OWNED THAT LIT UP A ROOM, AND REDISCOVER YOUR PASSION. BE DELIBERATE. DO NOT ALLOW LIFE TO PLACE YOU ON THE HAMSTER WHEEL, WHERE YOU'RE RUNNING AND GETTING NOWHERE. DON'T LOSE YOU AND IF YOU ALREADY HAVE, HAVE THE COURAGE TO GET FIND YOURSELF AGAIN!!

DEVOTIONAL:

YOUR CURRENT SITUATION MAY BE A MODE OF TRANSPORTATION TO YOUR NEXT LEVEL IN DESTINY. WE OFTEN CONFUSE A BURDEN AND A BLESSING, OFTEN FORGETTING THEY BOTH HAVE A WEIGHT WE MUST CARRY. SO TAKE ANOTHER LOOK AT WHAT YOU'RE GOING THROUGH, YOUR PERCEPTION DETERMINES YOUR PERFORMANCE!!

SELF CHALLENGE:

TAKE ANOTHER LOOK AT YOUR SITUATION. HOW CAN I MAKE THIS BURDEN A BLESSING?

_____

_____

HAVING THOSE AROUND YOU THAT KNOW YOUR WEAKNESS, BUT STILL RESPECT YOUR STRENGTHS IS PRICELESS!

DEVOTIONAL:

CHERISH THOSE THAT KNOW YOUR WEAKNESSES BUT STILL SEE YOU AS STRONG. WE ALL FALL SHORT IN CERTAIN AREAS OF OUR LIVES, SOME MORE THAN OTHERS. HAVING THOSE AROUND YOU THAT KNOW YOUR WEAKNESS, BUT STILL RESPECT YOUR STRENGTHS IS PRICELESS. VALUE THOSE THAT DO NOT ALLOW YOUR WEAKNESS TO DETERMINE HOW YOU'RE TREATED. IT'S NOT ABOUT CONDONING OR ENABLING; IT'S ABOUT CELEBRATING EACH OTHER'S STRENGTH IN SPITE OF OUR WEAKNESSES. SO LOVE AS YOU WANT TO BE LOVED AND DON'T BE QUICK TO JUDGE, BECAUSE AS AWESOME AND BRILLIANT AS YOU ARE, YOU TOO HAVE A WEAKNESS OR TWO....

SELF-CHECK:

THE MOST FLAWED PERSON, IS ALSO AN ANSWER TO SOMEONE'S PRAYER. HAVE YOU FOCUSED TO MUCH ON THEIR WEAKNESSES?

_____

_____

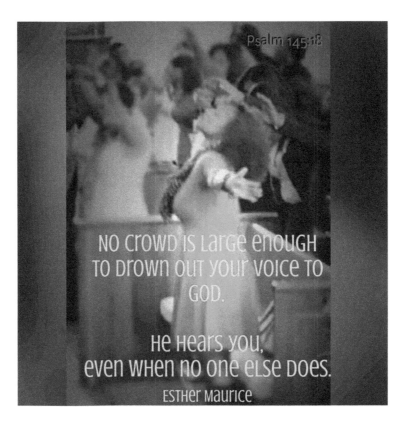

Psalm 145:18

NO CrOWD IS LARGE ENOUGH
TO DROWN OUT YOUR VOICE TO
GOD.

HE HEARS YOU,
EVEN WHEN NO ONE ELSE DOES.
ESTHER MAURICE

DEVOTIONAL

NEVER FORGET THAT YOUR VOICE IS HEARD. A WHISPER OR A SHOUT, HE'S
ALWAYS LISTENING. PRAY SO THAT YOU MAY RECEIVE YOUR ANSWER!

SELF-CHALLENGE:

SPEND SOME QUIET, UNINTERRUPTED TIME WITH GOD

DON'T DESPISE THE HURT YOU HAVE EXPERIENCED. MANY HAVE LEFT US SCARRED BUT YOUR SCARS ARE A REMINDER OF THE EXPERIENCE AND EVIDENCE OF YOUR ABILITY TO HEAL.

ESTHER MAURICE

John 20:27

DEVOTIONAL:

THERE IS A STORY BEHIND EACH SCAR THAT YOU CARRY. IT'S A REMINDER OF THE EXPERIENCE, THE PAIN AND MORE IMPORTANTLY YOUR ABILITY TO HEAL. YOUR PAIN IS NOT IN VAIN. YOUR SCARS ARE YOUR EVIDENCE THAT YOU SURVIVED!

JOHN 20:27

SELF-CHECK:

ARE YOU SO CONSUMED WITH THE WOUND THAT YOU HAVE PREVENTED YOUR OWN HEALING?

_____

_____

SHHHHH...

DEVOTIONAL

Unfortunately we have come to a time when those that can be trusted are few and far in between. Often times those that betray your trust have never been able to receive authentic love. The kind of Love that protects, covers and respects discretion. So how do you handle that?? ...keep being you, show love but be silent about what you don't want shared. Your silence has a voice.

SELF-CHECK:

Are you a safe place? Can you be trusted?

_____

_____

DEVOTIONAL:

PATIENCE.

TIMING IS EVERYTHING. GETTING WHAT YOU WANT AT THE WRONG TIME ISN'T A BLESSING. TODAY I PRAY YOUR STRENGTH TO WAIT FOR WHAT YOU DESERVE AND YOU DON'T WASTE TIME CHASING WHAT YOU CAN ATTRACT!

DEVOTIONAL:

TAKE ANOTHER LOOK!!

WE GIVE OUR "HATERS" SO MUCH ATTENTION THAT WE OVERLOOK THE ONES THAT CHEER US ON! TODAY TAKE A LOOK AROUND YOU, YOU'LL BE SURPRISED TO SEE THE PEOPLE THAT WANT TO SEE YOU WIN OUTNUMBER THOSE THAT WANT YOU TO LOSE!

Dear Lord,

Today let me hide your word in my heart. The vault is where my riches, my wisdom, my strength, my joy, and my wealth is hidden. The vault that never goes bankrupt but is replenished day after day as I read and study your Word. I deposit into my heavenly bank, which I have been given earthly access.

Thank you Lord that even though my credit and past were not befitting to be approved, you stood in the gap and signed on my behalf. You validated me. You approved me. You have me the access code that I may walk freely in and out of this vault without question. Thank you. Amen.

DEVOTIONAL:

YOU ARE RICHER THAN YOU THINK!!

SELF CHECK:

HAVE YOU UNDERESTIMATED THE VALUE OF YOUR ACCESS?

Having pure intentions or a pure heart does not exempt you from being hurt. The real challenge in life is maintaining a pure heart in the midst of all the hurt.

Esther Maurice

Proverbs 4:23

DEVOTIONAL:

HAVING PURE INTENTIONS OR A PURE HEART DOES NOT EXEMPT YOU FROM BEING HURT. THE REAL CHALLENGE IN LIFE IS MAINTAINING A PURE HEART IN THE MIDST OF ALL THE HURT. GUARDING IT AGAINST THE VAPORS OF DECEPTION, THE VENOM OF BETRAYAL AND THE SHADOWS OF HATE. YOUR PURE HEART DOES NOT ALWAYS GUARANTEE HONESTY, LOYALTY OR LOVE. BE HONEST AND HUMBLE ENOUGH TO CHECK YOUR MOTIVES AND INTENTIONS WHILE REFUSING TO ALLOW YOUR HEART TO BE A HOSTAGE OF HURT. YOUR DESTINY DEPENDS ON YOUR LIBERATION!

SELF CHECK:

WHAT HURT HAS BEEN KEEPING YOUR HOSTAGE?

_____

_____

So many of us require loyalty, Yet, so few of us give it.

DEVOTIONAL:

So many of us require loyalty yet, so few of us give it. To be loyal there has to be some level of love and/ or respect. This love and respect is founded on trust. Trust is feeling secure that the very thing that you are loyal to will not only be loyal to you, but will also follow through on the promises you believe you will see from it. Often times loyalty is absent because trust isn't present. After being hurt numerous times, our trust can become a hostage of our hurt. So I challenge you today, to check your heart. Don't allow hurt to blur your vision where trust and loyalty never seem to be present. Be prudent, but dare to trust again. You need others to walk this journey with you. There are still loyal ones out there!

SELF-CHECK:

What are the conditions of your loyalty? Be Honest.

_____

_____

Transition

DEVOTIONAL:

WHEN TRANSITIONING INTO YOUR NEW SEASON TO BETTER YOURSELF, DO NOT BE ALARMED IF YOU BECOME UNRECOGNIZABLE TO THOSE CLOSEST TO YOU. RENEWED MINDS PRODUCE NEW BEHAVIOR; NEW SPEECH AND REINVIGORATED THOUGHTS. GIVE THEM A CHANCE TO GET TO KNOW THE NEW YOU. YOU MUST ACCEPT THAT ONLY SOME OF THEM MAY GROW WITH YOU, BUT, IT'S OK BECAUSE EVERYONE IS NOT MEANT TO GO WITH YOU. KEEP MOVING FORWARD. PRAYERS ARE ANSWERED DURING TRANSITION PERIODS AS WELL.

SELF-CHECK:

HAVE THOSE AROUND MENTIONED HOW MUCH YOU HAVE CHANGED? HAVE YOU? HOW SO?

_____

_____

"I WAS WRONG",
"I'M SORRY",
"I APOLOGIZE".
SIMPLE WORDS THAT
CAN SOLVE THE MOST
COMPLICATED SITUATIONS.

DEVOTIONAL:

. HAVING THE COURAGE TO BE HUMBLE ENOUGH TO SEEK PEACE IS A BY-PRODUCT OF MATURITY. HAVE WE BECOME SO SELF-CENTERED, SELFISH AND DARE I SAY, ARROGANT THAT WE'VE LOST ALL SENSE OF COMPASSION AND EMPATHY? WE OFTEN LOOK BACK OVER SITUATIONS & REALIZE WHAT WE COULD AND WOULD DO DIFFERENTLY, BUT ONCE PRESENTED WITH THE SITUATION AGAIN, OUR REACTION REMAINS THE SAME. DARE TO BE HONEST TODAY. HONEST WITH YOURSELF ABOUT WHO YOU HAVE BECOME AND WHO YOU WANT TO BE. HUMILITY CHALLENGES YOU TO SEEK PEACE INSTEAD OF VICTORY, BUT WISDOM REVEALS THAT THEY'RE THE SAME.

SELF-CHALLENGE:

HOW WILL YOU USE THESE SIMPLE WORDS TODAY?

_____

_____

DEVOTIONAL:

SOMETIMES IT FEELS LIKE THE FILTERS WE USE IN OUR PICTURES AND SOCIAL MEDIA POSTINGS HAVE SLIPPED INTO OUR EVERYDAY LIVES. IMAGES EDITED TO REFLECT WHAT WORKS BEST AT THE TIME. WHAT WE THINK LOOKS GOOD. BUT, RARELY DO WE SEE THE REAL, UNFILTERED, AUTHENTIC PICTURE OF WHAT TRULY EXISTS; WHO WE REALLY ARE. WE SMILE WHEN WE FACE THEM AND ROLL OUR EYES WHEN THEY TURN AWAY. WE ACT IS IF WE CARE AND WHEN WE THINK NO ONE IS LISTENING, WE COMPLAIN. SOME MAY SAY, IT HELPS KEEPS THINGS IN BALANCE. IT VERY WELL MAY DO SO, BUT REMEMBER BALANCE REQUIRES AN EVEN DISTRIBUTION TO KEEP THE OTHER SIDE FROM FALLING. SO THE SAME INAUTHENTIC, FILTERED, JADED REALITY YOU PRESENT, YOU ARE GETTING IT BACK. ALL FOR THE SAKE OF BALANCE. BE HONEST WITH SOMEONE!

OUR FAITH DOES NOT RELEASE US OF THE RESPONSIBILITY TO DO SOMETHING IT INITIATES IT!!

DEVOTIONAL:

YOUR FAITH IN GOD DOES NOT RELEASE YOU OF THE RESPONSIBILITY TO DO YOUR PART. GOD HAS EMPOWERED YOU TO ACCOMPLISH THE VERY THING THAT YOUR PURSUE. IF YOU TRULY BELIEVE THAT YOU ARE AN ANSWERED PRAYER, GET TO WORK AND BE READY TO RESPOND!

You won't have to Announce the Obvious...

DEVOTIONAL:

BECAUSE OF OUR FAITH IN GOD, SOMETIMES WE INADVERTENTLY FIND OURSELVES IN SITUATIONS THAT ARE BEYOND OUR CONTROL. AS A RESULT, YOU CAN BE VIEWED AS UNREALISTIC, CRAZY, STUPID, IGNORANT, BLIND, CONFUSED...AND THE LIST GOES ON. DON'T WORRY, YOU DON'T HAVE TO EXPLAIN YOUR WAY OUT OF IT. THEY MAY DOUBT YOUR PROCESS BUT WILL LEARN TO HAVE FAITH FOR YOUR MIRACLE. FAITH IT FAITHFULLY!

HEBREWS 11:6

A WHISPER OR A SHOUT

GOD

IS ALWAYS LISTENING

Psalm 55:22

DEVOTIONAL:

WE CAN'T CONTROL EVERYTHING. THAT CERTAINLY INCLUDES PEOPLE AND THEIR THOUGHTS OF YOU. SOME OF US CAN BARELY CONTROL OURSELVES. INSTEAD OF STRESSING ABOUT HOW TO RUN & HANDLE THE SITUATION TODAY, IET'S LEARN AND USE THE POWER OF OUR VOICE TO GOD. HE HEARS AND HE'S LISTENING. CAST ALL YOUR CARES TO HIM BECAUSE HE IS TRULY THE ONE IN CONTROL. PSALM 55:22

PAY ATTENTION TO THOSE AROUND YOU
THEIR GIFTS, TALENTS, WISDOM &
PERSONALITIES
THEY MAY BE AN ANSWER TO YOUR
PRAYER
IN MORE WAYS THAN ONE.
#THEYARETHEANSWERTOAPRAYER

DEVOTIONAL:

BE DELIBERATE IN FINDING THE ANSWER TO YOUR PRAYER. IT'S CLOSER THAN YOU THINK!

ACTION PLAN:

MAKE A LIST OF THOSE AROUND YOU AND THEIR GIFTS.

Your smile, Your hugs,
Your encouraging words,
your personality,
your sense of humor, your love--
a list of the valuable things you can give
away and still never run out.
#BeTheAnswerToSomeonesPrayer
#YoureValuable

THEY RE-PLACE YOU
BEFORE
THEY REPLACE YOU.

DEVOTIONAL:

BE WISE ENOUGH TO ASSESS YOUR RELATIONSHIPS.

OFTEN TIMES WE ARE REPOSITIONED, BEFORE WE ARE REPLACED. MOVED OUT OF THE SPACE WE ONCE OCCUPIED TO MAKE ROOM FOR ANOTHER. THIS HAPPENS WITH WORK, FRIENDSHIPS AND RELATIONSHIPS. BUT I CHALLENGE YOU TO CONSIDER SEVERAL THINGS AS TO WHY ARE YOU BEING REPOSITIONED? WHAT IS THE MOTIVE BEHIND IT AND IS IT NECESSARILY A BAD THING?

BEING REPOSITIONED TO BE REPLACED CAN BE PREPARATION FOR PROMOTION, JUST BE HONEST WITH YOURSELF OF THE MOTIVES. KNOWING WHERE YOU STAND IS IMPORTANT TO KNOW HOW YOU SHOULD MOVE FORWARD.

CHANGE IS NOT ALWAYS EASY BUT OFTEN TIMES NECESSARY.

DO NOT WITHHOLD GOOD
FROM THOSE WHO NEED IT,
WHEN YOU HAVE THE ABILITY TO HELP.
PROVERBS 3:27

DEVOTIONAL:

ONE OF THE TOUGHEST DECISIONS TO MAKE IS TO HELP SOMEONE THAT HAS HURT YOU. THEIR NEED FOR HELP OFTEN TIMES FEELS LIKE THE PERFECT PUNISHMENT FOR THEIR OFFENSE AGAINST YOU. YOU SOMEHOW FEEL JUSTIFIED FOR YOUR PAIN, BY THEIR NEED FOR HELP. BUT I CHALLENGE YOU TODAY, IF YOU'RE ABLE TO HELP SOMEONE, HELP THEM. DON'T ALLOW YOUR HEART OR EGO TO BECOME SO JADED WITH PAIN THAT YOU LOSE COMPASSION. THIS MAY NOT BE TO TEST YOUR CHARACTER, BUT TO REVEAL IT.

YOU DON'T WITHHOLD HELP BECAUSE OF WHAT THEY'VE DONE, YOU HELP BECAUSE OF WHO YOU ARE! YOU ARE THE ANSWER TO SOMEONE'S PRAYER, EVEN TO THOSE THAT MAY HAVE WRONGED YOU. STAND TALL BY BEING HUMBLE ENOUGH TO HELP. LOVE ALWAYS WINS.

Rejection usually comes from the counterfeit, Before selection for the authentic.

<u>DEVOTIONAL:</u>

We often seek acceptance from the wrong place. Rejection can leave you feeling hurt, worthless, and cause you to question everything about yourself. Today I challenge you to re-consider those emotions, you're valuable and someone is asking God for who you are right now, even at this point in your life.

You're someone's Answer.

SOMEONE WOKE UP THIS MORNING

AND

PRAYED FOR YOU.

#YouAreTheAnswerToSomeonesPrayer

DEVOTIONAL:

GET INTO POSITION, THEY ARE LOOKING FOR YOU!

"LOVE CAUSES US TO HOLD ON SO TIGHT BUT CAN ALSO REQUIRE US TO LET GO."

DEVOTIONAL:

YOU CAN'T CONTROL PEOPLE'S THOUGHTS, DECISIONS, PERCEPTIONS, ACTIONS OR REACTIONS, BUT WHAT YOU CAN CONTROL IS YOU. WE ALLOW SO MUCH IN THE NAME OF LOVE THAT OFTEN TIMES OUR GENUINE LOVE FOR OTHERS AFFECT HOW WE LOVE OURSELVES. BE COMMITTED WITHOUT BEING CONSUMED. IT DOESN'T MEAN LOVE IS LOST. IT'S BECAUSE OF LOVE SOMETIMES YOU HAVE TO LET GO AND ALLOW OTHERS TO GROW OR AT THE VERY LEAST LEARN TO APPRECIATE THE IRREPLACEABLE THINGS IN LIFE.

The most trying circumstances will take you from talking ABOUT god and have you speaking TO God.

DEVOTIONAL:

Sometimes you have to go through the valley to get to the appointed table set for you. These are the circumstances that take you from talking ABOUT God and have you speaking TO God.

There may be shadows in the valley, but remember that the shadow is never present without light and the projection of the shadow is always bigger than the actual object. You only see the shadow because the light (God) is with you. So. that thing that you're so afraid of, is not as big as it seems.

Besides, the Shepard that you trusted in the green pastures is with you in the valley. Don't stray, the journey isn't over yet & you are not alone.

Psalm 23

MANY MAY DOUBT YOUR PROCESS,
BUT WILL LEARN THE POWER OF FAITH BECAUSE OF YOUR MIRACLE.
PHILIPPIANS 3:14-15

DEVOTIONAL:

IT'S ABOUT YOUR FAITH, NOT THEIRS.
BE BOLD ENOUGH TO STAND.

PHILIPPIANS 3:14-15

Defining moments...
They may have
called you
by your situation,
but soon
they will call you
by your miracle.

#NameChange
Isaiah 43:19
@thesthermaurice

DEVOTIONAL:

THEY WILL ALWAYS LOOK AND THEY WILL ALWAYS TALK,
BUT WHAT THEY ARE SAYING IS ABOUT TO CHANGE! I

Wanting to quit, isn't a sign of weakness,
It's a reminder that you're human.

Having those in your life that won't let you quit,
is a reminder that you're loved.
#DontGiveUp

DEVOTIONAL:

You've come too far to quit!!

DEVOTIONAL:

It's amazing how God shields us even when we feel we are at our lowest;
others see otherwise.

"You never know How God is revealing himself to your enemy through you and your experience."

#AfterTheSmokeClears
#YoureIgnitedNotConsumed

@thesthermaurice

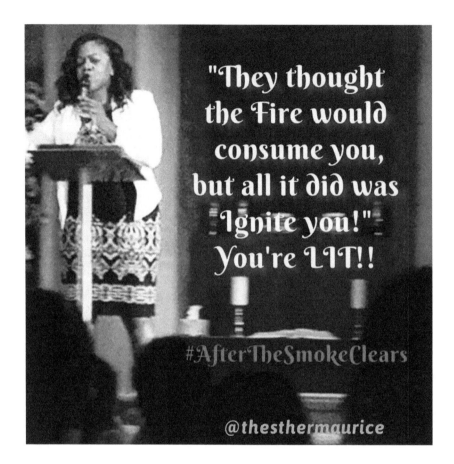

"They thought the Fire would consume you, but all it did was Ignite you!" You're LIT!!

#AfterTheSmokeClears

@thesthermaurice

DEVOTIONAL:

AFTER THE SMOKE CLEARS, YOU WON'T BE ASHES, YOU'LL BE THE FLAME!!

DANIEL 3

SELF CHECK:

DO YOU FEEL CONSUMED?

_____

_____

Make Today
one of those days
You brag about tomorrow!!
#BeGreat

DEVOTIONAL:

Stay Focused!!

Philippians 1:6

DEVOTIONAL

FROM LOSING A LOVED ONE, A FAILED RELATIONSHIP OR DISAPPOINTMENT, A BROKEN HEART FEELS LIKE THE WORLD IS COMING TO AN END. BUT THE HEART IS THE ONLY PART OF US THAT CAN BE CONSTANTLY BROKEN WITHOUT EVER SKIPPING A BEAT. IT BEATS BECAUSE IT'S ALIVE BUT YOU LIVE BECAUSE YOU HAVE THE CAPACITY TO HEAL. SO TODAY, I PRAY THAT GOD'S LOVE HEALS YOUR HEART FROM THE PAIN OF BEING BROKEN AND THAT YOU EMBRACE THE FACT THAT THE WORLD DID NOT END, BUT A HEALED HEART BRINGS ABOUT A NEW BEGINNING.

PSALM 73:26

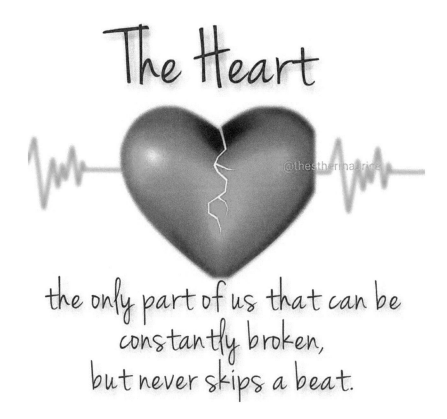

The Heart

the only part of us that can be constantly broken, but never skips a beat.

THE
VOICE OF DISTRACTION
IS ALWAYS
FAMILIAR.

DEVOTIONAL:

STAY FOCUSED, DISTRACTIONS USUALLY COME FROM THE THINGS AND PEOPLE THAT ARE CLOSEST TO US.

SELF −CHALLENGE:

NAME THE PEOPLE WHO HAVE THE POWER TO DISTRACT YOU.

_____

_____

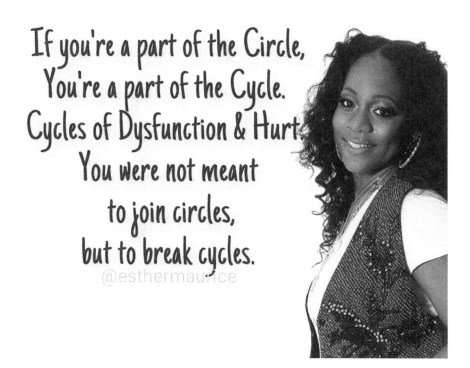

If you're a part of the Circle,
You're a part of the Cycle.
Cycles of Dysfunction & Hurt.
You were not meant
to join circles,
but to break cycles.
@esthermaurice

DEVOTIONAL

THERE'S A REASON YOU DON'T FIT IN. BE THE CHANGE YOU WANT TO SEE!!

YOU DESERVE TO BE LOVED.

DEVOTIONAL:

Sometimes we are so accustomed to being loved with conditions that pure, genuine and unconditional love feels foreign. It's uncomfortable. But I challenge you today to embrace the notion that you deserve to be loved, unconditionally. Don't allow past hurts, betrayal and bad motives cause you to sabotage something you think is too good to be true.

You Deserve to be Happy.

DEVOTIONAL

Many of us aren't happy because we let others tell us what should make us happy. But I challenge you today to find your own joy. The person, the place or thing that not only makes you smile on the outside but makes your heart smile, just because. You deserve to be happy, even when others think otherwise.

You Deserve the Best.

DEVOTIONAL:

WE DON'T HAVE THE BEST BECAUSE WE DON'T DEMAND THE BEST. THERE'S NOTHING WRONG WITH SETTING A STANDARD FOR THE THINGS YOU WANT. YOU DON'T HAVE TO SETTLE.

IT'S ABOUT YOUR FAITH NOT THEIRS.

DEVOTIONAL:

YOU DON'T NEED ANYONE'S PERMISSION TO BELIEVE WHAT GOD PLACED ON YOUR HEART. TOO OFTEN WE TRY TO CONVINCE OTHERS TO SUPPORT WHAT WE HAVE FAITH FOR. IT'S YOUR MISSION, NOT THEIRS. IT'S YOUR DREAM, NOT THEIRS. IT'S YOUR FAITH, NOT THEIRS! NOW, GO, BE GREAT!

DEVOTIONAL

WHEN YOU KNOW WHO YOU ARE, WHO YOU WERE CREATED TO BE AND WHAT YOU WANT, YOUR DECISIONS AND DETERMINATION FOLLOW THAT DIRECTION. NOTHING IS MORE POWERFUL THAN A RENEWED MIND.

PHILLIPPIANS 2:5

THERE'S NOTHING MORE POWERFUL THAN A RENEWED MIND.

LIFE OFTEN THROWS SO MUCH AT US, ALL AT ONCE. NO MATTER WHAT MAY HAVE YOU OVERWHELMED TODAY, I PRAY YOU RECEIVE THE PEACE OUR LORD HAS ALREADY GIVEN US. YOU MAY NOT KNOW ALL THE ANSWERS, BUT LEARN TO TRUST THE ONE THAT DOES.

TRUST GOD.

Thank you for saying "No".

We thank Him for what we receive, but also thank Him for the things, people and circumstances he blocked. #GodisAlwaysinControl #Thankful #EMM

DEVOTIONAL:

His unconditional love,
His unmerited favor,
His abounding Grace,
My hallelujah belongs to God.
He deserves it.

SELF -CHALLENGE

Today, tell God all the things you are thankful for.

DEVOTIONAL:

People are intimated and feel threatened by you for different reasons. You can't understand why, because it's not about you, it's about them and what they lack. So stop trying to change those that are jealous of you. Pray that they see their own potential and all the brilliant gifts and talents they possess. Go on, Be Great!

My Hallelujah Belongs to You.

@esthermaurice

JEALOUSY IS NOT ABOUT WHAT YOU HAVE, IT'S ABOUT WHAT "THEY" LACK.

DEVOTIONAL:

It's wise to think before you respond. Many quick responses have wrecked relationships. Responding from anger, confusion or hurt, blurs your vision. So be still, just listen. The more you listen the less you will have to say. More importantly, you will know then exactly what to say.

James 1:19

DEVOTIONAL:

LIFE HAS A WAY OF REMINDING US TO FOCUS ON WHAT IS TRULY IMPORTANT. LEARN FROM YOUR PAST BUT LIVE IN YOUR PRESENT SO YOU CAN LEAP TOWARD YOUR FUTURE. THERE'S SO MUCH MORE AHEAD OF YOU! GO, BE GREAT!

PHILIPPIANS 3:14

DEVOTIONAL:

One thing you can choose to control is your reaction. Everything will not always go as you planned or as you hoped, but instead of worrying I challenge you to choose to have peace no matter what happens. Trust God for whatever you face today. Go, Be great!

@thesthermaurice

DETERMINED.

Making a decision & having the Discipline to stick to it! #fearless

DEVOTIONAL:

The journey builds character! Phillipians 4:13

Lightning Source UK Ltd.
Milton Keynes UK
UKHW051823260219
338072UK00007B/118/P